FOR THE LOVE OF BRISKET

FOR THE LOVE OF BRISKET

How to Smoke a Barbecue Brisket Texas-Style

JOHN W. DAVIS

DEDICATION

I would like to dedicate this book to my beautiful wife, Ana Davis, and my father, Howard Lee Davis. Ana, I knew the first time I saw you that I loved you. I thank you from the bottom of my heart for loving me and coming into my life. I asked God many times to send me someone I could love. My prayers were answered. Dad, thank you for giving me your name and choosing me to be your son. You will always be my rock and my foundation. You were the best father a son could ask for. You will never be forgotten.

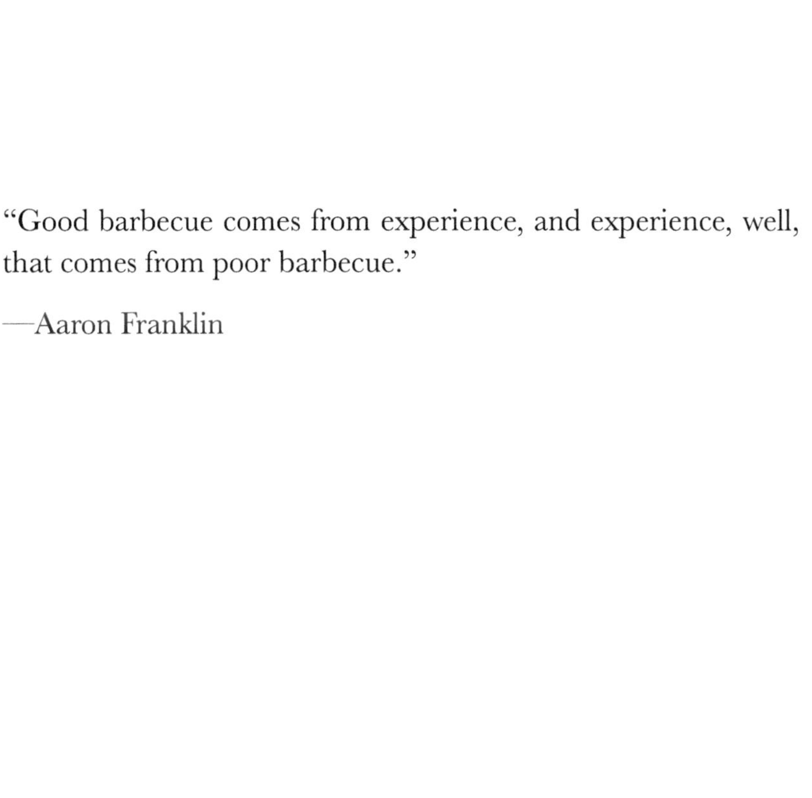

"Good barbecue comes from experience, and experience, well, that comes from poor barbecue."

—Aaron Franklin

CONTENTS

INTRODUCTION

Smoked Barbecue Brisket

I can honestly say anyone who takes the time to make a savory BBQ brisket is someone who loves the togetherness it brings to friends and family. BBQ in general, in my opinion, is a labor of love. I don't consider myself an expert at all. I'm not a world-renowned top chef that has their own cooking show or YouTube Channel.

I can say over the years, through trial and error, I have learned how to cook/smoke a great BBQ brisket. I decided to write this book for the common Joe and Jill who wants to cook a brisket for his or her family and friends.

The common backyard griller does not want to guess the type of meat to buy, the time it takes to cook the brisket, the temperature you should be cooking at, blah, blah, blah. I do know a little more about cooking brisket and other BBQ meats than the average Joe or Jill. With that said, I would like to share my experiences with you and explain to you how a Texas woman named Ana changed my life and took me to visit her family down in the Rio Grande Valley.

It was there in the "Valley" where I became fascinated with Texas-style brisket. I will explain to you in detail how I ended up not only learning how to cook in general but also learning how to prepare one of the best beef dishes you can buy. I'm hoping after you have read my story, you will come to love brisket as much as I do.

I have been blessed to have this opportunity to share my story with you. I am hoping my journey down memory lane will bring happiness to your heart and bring you closer to your loved ones and family friends. I just want to provide a few simple suggestions on how to smoke a Texas-style barbecue brisket with confidence, but at the same time, make the process simple and direct.

I am not going to talk about the history of brisket, but I will mention that brisket originated as a Jewish cuisine. The history of brisket is fascinating to me and something every BBQ connoisseur should know.

We all can learn so much from so many other cultures. This is what makes America such a great nation. The cooking methods for cooking brisket have changed over the years in so many ways. Barbecue brisket has become one of the star dishes in the barbecue world. If you can smoke a brisket to perfection, you can cook anything.

The history of brisket is especially important, and every BBQ lover should look at the history to see how this style of cooking was created.

The bottom line is beef brisket is here to stay, and people love eating great smoked brisket. My background is simple.

I have learned through trial and error how to cook many barbecue dishes. My dad, my inspiration and foundation, was a cook, among other duties in the Navy. My dad would survive World War II and stay in the Navy for over twenty (20) years. I will talk more about my dad, Howard Lee Davis, later in this book. I learned at an early age how to cook. It was normal for me to help prepare breakfast, lunch, or dinner for my foster brothers and sisters at the Davis residence.

I learned at an early age not to overcook steak. My dad always cooked his steak to medium rare and would tell me, "If you cook a steak over medium rare, you've just ruined a good steak." This was my father's philosophy. In general, if you purchase a steak, you can prepare it any way you want—you are the one eating the steak.

My father's tools of the trade were a black, cast-iron skillet over a high flame. The pan had to be hot, and the oil had to be hot. The pan was so hot I could hear the steak being seared at a high temperature. A pinch of salt, some A1 steak sauce, and that was it. I watched my father cook on many occasions.

My Dad. Howard Lee Davis.

All I remember were the functions and many gatherings after church that normally involved cooking on Saturday and serving meals on Sunday after church. Every Sunday, we would go to Bethel Baptist Church on Clay Street. Reverend Hampton was our preacher. I was always dressed in my Sunday best. Black dress shoes, collared shirt, and a jacket with a tie. We would head to church around 7:30 am.

I would go to Sunday school and then walk over to the room where the children's choir practice was located. By 11:30 am, we were in the main church listening to the pastor preach. Growing up in a Baptist church, I knew I better not act up in church, or I would get that pinch on the thigh by my mom. You better not yell out when you are getting pinched, and you better not cry.

When the sermon was over, and we walked out of church, I was afraid I would be struck down by lightning if I did anything wrong. I sang a solo of "How Great Thou Art" one Sunday. I could see the pride on my parents' faces when I sang in church. I also knew when the collection plate was about to go around.

Howard Lee Davis. SD2 US Navy World War II and Korea. Born July 1920. Died Dec 1993.

The church choir would get loud, and the preacher would start talking about the needs of the church and the needy. I did notice the offering plate would go around more than once sometimes.

I was directed by my mother to put the fifty (50) cents I was given by my dad into the collection plate when the basket came around. I was thinking fifty (50) cents could buy me some ice cream when I got out of the church.

I thought to myself, "God would not get mad at me if I bought myself some ice cream." Sometimes, I would put my fifty (50) cents inside the basket, but sometimes, well, I did not. The cookouts provided by the church were immense. There were pounds of fried chicken cooked with macaroni and cheese.

The dinner plates consisted of fried chicken, macaroni and cheese, corn on the cob, baked beans, collard greens, sweet potatoes (aka Yams) and cornbread. I have not even mentioned the various desserts being provided.

Sister Bell would make this peach cobbler that was out of this world. I wish I had Sister Bell's recipe today. I never arrived home on time to go outside and play with my friends. Church was an all-day thing on some Sundays.

Unfortunately, I would lose my mother to cancer at the age of thirteen (13) and watch my dad just lose his love for cooking and life in general. The night my mother died, she asked me to call my dad because she was not feeling well. My dad, at the time, was a security guard assigned to the 32nd Street Naval Station.

I called my dad and told him over the phone mom needed him home because she was not feeling well. I jumped into bed with my mom and asked my mom what was wrong. My mom held me close and told me she was going to heaven tonight, and she wanted me to be happy for her. My mom said in the morning she would see the glory of heaven, and she would always look over me to make sure I was safe.

My mom explained to me that if I were ever in trouble, I should pray, and she and God would be at my side to help me. My mother then asked me not to cry at her funeral. I did not understand why my mom was telling me all these things.

My mom said she was not feeling well, but she looked fine to me. As I continued to talk to my mom, I could see her face glow, and she smiled as she talked to me. My mom had this sense of peace.

It did not appear she was in any pain or had any discomfort. I did not understand what I was seeing at the time. My mom was preparing to see God, and she knew in her heart that she was going home. If you're a Christian and you believe in God, like I do, you will understand exactly what I'm trying to say.

My dad arrived home and took my mom to Kaiser Hospital on Zion Road. I stayed with the next-door neighbor, Miss Rickman, across the street. The next morning, my mom was gone. I did not cry at my mom's funeral because I made a promise not to cry.

During the funeral, so many people came up to me to give me their condolences. It was during this time people would ask me why I was not crying for my mom. It was so hard not to cry, but I made a promise to my mom, and I was going to keep it.

My dad was crying his eyes out, and all I could do was give my dad a hug. I told my dad everything was going to be okay. I did not know what else to say. I told my dad later, after the funeral, why I did not cry, and this only made my dad cry more.

I wish I had not told my dad about the promise I made to mom. I became angry inside and asked God why he would take my mom away if he was so great. My mom did everything to worship God, and God took her away. It was a rough time for me.

At that time of my life, you could say I lost my faith in God, and God and I were not friends anymore. I would learn later in life how untrue my statement was. As for the kids at school, most of them were kind, but others were cruel. I already had a bad temper and was always into fights. Being adopted did not help matters. I would hear it all the time. "Blackie," "Blackie," "Blackie."

You're a tar baby. Nobody wanted you. "Oh Black Johnny," "Bamba-lam." Your mom threw you in a trash can. You have to remember that this occurred in the mid-seventies (70s). Dark complexion brothas were getting no play. Not to mention, I was bald-headed because my dad would not let me grow a "natural" (Slang for Afro).

My dad would take me to the barbershop and say one (1) word. "Off." The Jackson 5 and lighter complexion brothas, like Howard Hewett in Shalamar and DeBarge, were the in thing at the time. The only dark-complexioned brotha who was getting all the play was Richard Roundtree, "Shaft."

That was a bad motha…You know the rest if you're from my age group. I remember being on the bus going to school, and my mom had recently died. This kid told me to cheer up because my mom was going to come back to life.

I turned around and told this kid to leave me alone. This kid was the neighborhood bully at the time. The kid then said, "Buy your mom some coast soap and wake your Mommy up." Everyone on the bus laughed.

That was some cold #$%^ to say. I wasn't laughing. I was filled with rage. A fight took place on the bus that day, and I was back in the principal's office again. At the time, there was a new bath soap called "Coast Soap" out on the market.

People using the soap in the commercials would shower and instantly be revived and refreshed. A terrible joke at my expense. My anger through the years only grew and became worse. I went through a phase where I would light various things on fire. I liked watching things burn. I will discuss that story in another book I will write in the future.

God willing. My dad had lost the love of his life. I had never seen my dad cry until my mom died. This was a couple who stayed together for thirty-five (35) years and made it through World War II. My dad would show me films of him out on a ship in the Pacific.

The ship was being tossed around by the sea as it was refueling. The waves were so high, but you could see servicemen still working on the deck of the ship doing their job. My dad would do a total of twenty-four (24) years in the Navy and had the rank of PO2/E5 when he retired from the military on July 30, 1962.

My dad did not talk about the war too much. The only time my dad would even mention World War II was when he watched the movie

"Patton." George C. Scott played Patton, and my dad would say, "If the leaders of the world at the time would have let Patton do his job, we would not have the problems we have today."

I did not know what he was talking about. I wanted to go outside and play. "Patton?" Who was "Patton?" As I grew older, I would understand what he meant. I believe my dad only stayed alive all those years after my mom died just to raise me.

My dad remarried when I was sixteen (16) years old and told me from day one he only remarried because he wanted to have someone home with me. My dad made it clear the love of his life was gone.

I still remember the night my dad asked me if he could die and go to heaven to see mom. I was twenty-eight (28) years old when my dad, at seventy-three (73) years old, asked me this question.

My dad was still calling me his little boy, and he told me he did not want to leave me because he knew I would be alone. I was able to tell my dad how much I loved him, and I thanked him for giving me his name. My dad said he was very proud of me because I served my country and became a San Diego Police Officer.

My dad said he was thankful I had never been arrested, and I always made him proud. With tears in my eyes, I told my dad he could go to mom, and I would be fine. I assured my dad I would be fine because he raised me the right way. I was working the 2nd watch patrol shift that night, so I was in my uniform when I came to visit my dad at Paradise Valley Hospital. I had to respond to a radio call, and I had to leave.

I told my dad I would be right back. I told my dad we could have lunch when I returned. My dad smiled and told me to do my job, but he had a different look on his face—a look I had never seen before. My dad was clearly proud of me, but like all parents, you always worry about your children no matter how old they get.

I was unable to return to the hospital due to numerous cover calls I had to respond to. I got off work at midnight and headed home. A few hours later, I received a call from the nurse to come back to the hospital because my dad did not have much longer to live.

I made it to the hospital, and as I was walking into the room, my dad died. When I walked into the room, I knew my dad was going to be fine. My dad's eyes were still open with a smile on his face as he looked up to the ceiling. I knew in my heart my dad was greeted by my mom, Viola, and taken home.

All I could hear in my mind was my solo in church, "How Great Thou Art." I closed my father's eyes and kissed him for the last time. I believe in my heart my dad was in a better place. To this day, my dad's spirit is always with me. There are times I smell his cologne out of nowhere. I just smile and say, "I'm okay, dad." "I'm okay."

My dad died in the month of December. My firstborn, who was only two (2) months old, also died in the month of December. I'm not a fan of December. The month of December can be depressing for me, but I keep my head up because the month of December is the month Christ was born. This is the real reason you're supposed to celebrate Christmas. People tend to forget that.

My stepmother, Miss Evil, I said to myself, was not a nice person, but she did know how to cook and owned her own restaurant at one time in her life. My stepmother had a college degree and worked on the Naval Station Base as a shipping clerk. My stepmother had a new car delivered to the house every two (2) years.

The stepmother would say, "I don't want a car older than two years old." "I don't want to deal with the maintenance." The dealership would drop off a light blue Lincoln Versailles, come pick up the older model, and return it to the dealership. The car dealer would kiss my stepmother's butt every two (2) years. The car being returned had less than 10K in mileage. It was a win-win for the dealership.

This lady would shop at Macy's and Nordstroms Department Store every weekend. I hated school shopping. Miss Evil would take me to the best stores to buy brand-new clothes for school. The neighbors thought she was such a good person.

If the neighbors could hear how this lady talked about them all behind their backs, they would have a different opinion. The mom that adopted me, Viola Davis, was a loving, God-fearing, soft-spoken woman.

I would hear my mom praying daily to God and thanking God for our blessings. My mother would read the bible along with this book called "The Daily Word." My mom prayed every day of her life.

If she was not praying for our family, she was praying for the sick and needy. I do not recall my parents ever arguing. If they argued, it was not in front of me.

I knew I could not come back to school the following year wearing the same clothes I wore the previous year. I would get clowned. The first day of school would arrive, and I would put on my new outfits and get ready to walk out the door.

Miss Evil would say, "Where are you going, Johnny? "I did not say you could wear those clothes to school." "Go back upstairs and wear something to school you wore last year." "I will let you know when you can wear the clothes I bought you."

Then she would have this grin on her face, waiting for me to beg and plead with her to let me wear my new clothes. Her grin looked just like the Grinch. I could not cuss her out like I wanted to.

Cussing was not permitted, and I was raised to know better. My dad would slap me down to the floor if I talked back to this evil lady. You can imagine what I wanted to say. I would walk out of the house and toward the bus stop wearing jeans that clearly were worn out.

The way this lady treated me would mold me into the strong person I am today. I said to myself, "I will do what I need to do on my own." "I do not depend on others." "I depend on myself and the Lord." My dad, on the other hand, had a sixth (6) grade education and had to drop out of school to help his father on the farm.

My dad enlisted in the Navy at eighteen (18) years old. My dad would send money home to his father and his baby sister Louise. My grandfather, Bill Davis, was a farmer in a small Texas town called Dime Box.

I never remember going without anything. My father was unable to pay for my college education, but my dad did provide me with the foundation I currently stand on. I started working shortly after my mom died. I would cut the neighbors' grass and pull weeds in the neighbors' garden.

I later had a paper route and worked for the Union-Tribune. I also washed cars at a rental car business by the airport. I did all these things so I could buy my own things. Later, at age sixteen (16), and throughout my teenage years, I would work at McDonalds, Jack in The Box, and Taco Bell.

It was all about getting the things I wanted without depending on my parents. I wanted to attend DeVry Institute when I graduated from high school. A representative from the DeVry Arizona Campus came to my home to talk with my father and Miss Evil about enrollment. The representative explained how DeVry had a new campus in Arizona, and I had good enough grades to attend.

My stepmother made it clear I was not her biological son, and it was not her responsibility to pay for my college. Unfortunately, everything my stepmother said was said in front of the school representative. This situation was so embarrassing to me. My dad had tears in his eyes and told me he was unable to help me go to trade school.

I told my dad it would be all right. I escorted this recruiter to his car and thanked him for coming by and telling me about the opportunity at DeVry Institute. I would later join the United States Army for the GI Bill so I could go to college.

The Army gave me 50K for college. Excuse me. Let me correct that last statement. I worked, sometimes, 20-hour days when I was assigned to my infantry unit. Yes, you can get by on only four (4) hours of sleep when the mission calls for it. The Army motto is, "In the Army, we do more before nine (9) AM than most people do all day." "This We'll Defend." The Army did not give me anything. I earned it.

PFC John Davis talking with PFC Flores over maintenance plans for a M113.

I did four (4) years of active service in Germany and four (4) years in the Army Reserve. I did it all on my own. An accomplishment of which I am immensely proud. I would advise any person who does not have a path to college to join any armed forces.

The military experience will change your life, and you will be able to experience things you would never have an opportunity to experience if you stayed on the block with the homies or home girls.

You also have pride in serving your country. When I left the military, I knew exactly what I wanted to do. I would return from Germany and attend DeVry Institute in the City of Industry (Pomona, California).

I would be the first Davis in my family to attend college. I enrolled in school and attended DeVry Institute for several months. A few months later, I received a phone call from my stepmother. My stepmother called me and informed me I needed to leave school because my dad had diabetes, and his left leg was going to be amputated down to his hip.

My stepmother, Cruella De Vil, in my mind, made it clear to me that if I did not drop school, she would put my father into a convalescent home because it was not her responsibility to take care of my father. I dropped out of school immediately and returned home to take care of my father. This is something I did gladly.

It was the least I could do for a man who adopted me and was always there for me whenever I needed him to be. My (M.O.S.) Military Occupational Specialty was a sixty-three (63) Tango (Systems Mechanic). In plain language, I was a heavy equipment (Tank) diesel mechanic.

I repaired M113 Personnel Carriers, the Bradley Fighting Vehicle (B.F.V.), the M1 Abrams Tank, and any other equipment in the motor pool that needed to be repaired. I came back to San Diego and found work as a mechanic immediately. I worked at a local Mobil Gas Station owned by a man named Kim. Kim stated that my military background as a mechanic made me overqualified for the job, but nevertheless, Kim gave me a job.

I was officially a Mobil Gas Station Attendant/Mechanic. Turning wrenches was a decent job that paid well. Kim would later help me rebuild the motor in my seventy-three (73) Super Beetle. The money I was making was okay, but I was getting tired of turning wrenches.

I wanted something more. The mayor of San Diego at the time, Maureen O'Connor, was hiring for the San Diego Police Department. The pay was excellent, and I was physically fit for the position.

I joined the San Diego Police Department and was promoted to the rank of detective after completing ten (10) years as a beat cop in Southeast San Diego. At that time, you had to work the streets/beat a number of years before you were promoted to the rank of detective. I would be told several times throughout my beat cop years that I was an asset to the community, and next time I would be promoted.

That was the way it was explained to me when I asked my captain at the time why I was not selected for investigations. I lived in the area where I worked, so I guess the department believed that made me an asset.

I can say, in my mind, it made me a target. I worked on numerous assignments as an investigator, such as Western Division Investigations, Night Vice, Sex Crimes, and, in my later years, Domestic Violence.

My favorite assignments were the Street Gang Unit and the FBI Violent Crimes Task Force Unit, Team 11. Team 11 investigated narcotic and gang activity in the Southeast area of San Diego, California. That is another story.

By the grace of God, I served thirty-one (31) years in the police department. I was grateful to be able to retire, and I pray every day for the officers who gave their lives to this noble profession.

It was during my last five (5) years working in the police department that I became fascinated with cooking various cuts of meat—especially barbecue brisket. I guess you can say a Texas woman, who I now call my wife, captured my curiosity for cooking brisket.

Officer John W. Davis. Miramar College, San Diego Police Academy, Class 120.

THE BASIC BACKYARD BBQ BACK IN THE DAY

Howard and Viola Davis.

I remember, as a child, my dad was outside firing up the grill. I would watch my father pour large amounts of fuel (gasoline) on top of some Kingsford Briquettes and light a match. "Stand back, Johnny," my dad would say.

I would watch this immense flame ignite through the grill grates. The flames were so high that the flames would touch the bottom branches of the tree we had in the middle of our backyard. My dad would look so proud as the flames grew higher and higher.

My Dad and Mom are having a happy moment together.

I would hear my mom yell to my dad, "Howard, isn't that fire a little too high? My dad would not even respond because I believe my father was hypnotized by the roaring flames about to catch the backyard tree on fire.

When my dad came out of his trance, he would tell mom he had everything under control. The backyard tree never burned down, so I guess it was all good. The smell.

That amazing smell of burning charcoal. That smell would never come close to the smell of burning mesquite. I would experience the scent of burning mesquite years later as an adult. Unfortunately, my dad would never have the opportunity to taste my very own BBQ brisket, but my father's fond memories of cooking will always live on through me.

My dad would have guests come over to the house from time to time. A typical gathering would consist of throwing some burgers and hot dogs on the grill for the kids. Of course, the adults attending the party would be given a nice, juicy steak. My dad requested a potluck so everyone at the party would be able to get a taste of their favorite dishes.

Growing up in Southern California, this was the norm for me. You either cooked BBQ in your backyard or you went to the beach and barbecued at the beach. Children, in general, did not walk into a room where adults were speaking.

I would get that look from my parents that gave me instructions on what I needed to do without my parents saying a word. Whatever the issue was, it could wait. The Davis household was a well-known foster home in the Emerald Hills Community. Our home was filled with several children who would later be adopted by loving families.

Some kids would only stay at the house for a short time. My mother would also babysit children in the neighborhood while their parents would work. I remember living with Bruce, Ronny, Beverly, and Ronald. Each child had a chore.

I would get the silverware while other children prepared the table by getting the dishes, cups, and chairs. Of course, this was the children's table. Children were not allowed to eat with adults. I would spend many of my younger years with my foster brother, Ronny.

Ronny and I were the last two (2) foster children left at the Davis household. Ronny was adopted, and I was left at the house alone.

Five (5) year service recognition award for caring for foster children to Howard and Viola Davis.

Several years would go by, and I would find myself setting a table for just me and the neighborhood friends who decided to come over to the house to visit during these birthday parties and cookouts. I was the lucky one. Mr. and Mrs. Davis decided to adopt me and give me their last name. I have honored the Davis name ever since.

I didn't realize I was adopted until the kid next door told me I was adopted. The kids were "basing" on each other one day and telling "Yo momma jokes." I told a good joke about my friend; I won't mention his name. The friend became angry. Then all I heard next was, "At least I'm not adopted, and I was not born in a trash can."

Adopted? What are you talking about? All the rest of the kids laughed, then joined in and started calling me adopted. I ran home in tears because this could not be. My dad was sitting on the porch in his rocking chair as he always did. I looked up at my father with tears in my eyes and asked him. Was I adopted?

My father smiled, picked me up, and placed me on his knee. My dad said, "Yes, son, you're adopted." "Your mother and I chose you to be our son." "Because we chose you, that makes you special." My dad then said the other kids were not chosen. Their parents had to take care of their nappy-headed behinds. I laughed, and this statement from my dad made me feel special.

I went back outside with my head raised high. The kids started in with the name-calling and saying I was adopted. I just explained I was special, and they were not. None of the kids mentioned I was adopted again, and we all went back to playing. No matter what was said between us kids, we always stayed friends to this day. I still love you. James.

Looking back on these fond memories, I didn't realize I had such a global-sized head as a child. I guess you could say I had a blockhead, just like Charlie Brown.

I was taught to answer the phone and say, "This is the Davis residence." "Johnny speaking." Look at that black phone. I know if you're my age, you remember the black phone.

I don't recall eating brisket growing up. Maybe a steak from time to time and a hamburger. I really did not get into BBQ brisket for many years. I began my fascination with BBQ when I met my wife Ana, who was originally from the Rio Grande Valley in the great state of Texas.

When I finally had my first bite of BBQ brisket, I can say I was hooked. I was fascinated with the way the meat was selected, seasoned, and prepared. I would learn so many ways to cook a BBQ brisket. My journey to learn how to cook a Texas BBQ Brisket began in the Rio Grande Valley of Mission, Texas.

Sitting with Mom and Dad after a dinner party.

MY WIFE'S FAMILY GATHERINGS IN THE RIO GRANDE VALLEY, MISSION, TEXAS

I was invited to my wife's childhood home in Mission, Texas, to meet her family. I had never even heard of Mission Texas, but I was told Mission Texas was in the heart of the Rio Grande Valley. Better known as the "R.G.V.," I met my wife Ana in 2008 on eHarmony. Yes, eHarmony.

eHarmony really works if you're serious about having a committed relationship. It was definitely a match in heaven. I was over 240 lbs. when I met Ana, and I loved to eat. When people ask me what our relationship is like, I tell them I'm Shrek, and my wife is the princess.

Ana and I had been dating for several months, and Ana wanted me to meet her mom and her eight (8) siblings. My wife's mom was still alive, but Ana's dad had passed on before I was able to meet him. I still remember walking into the room to meet not only Ana's mom but Ana's brothers and one (1) sister.

Ana has a total of seven (7) brothers. Yes, seven (7) brothers. Several brothers arrived at the house to greet me. These Texas men were standing there staring at me with their cowboy boots, large Texas hats, and large Texas belt buckles, too. I'm a California, Southeast, San Diego guy. "No one from my neighborhood wore cowboy hats and boots. Not in my hood. The only time I have ever seen a cowboy hat and boots was while I was watching a John Wayne movie. I realized real quick there were not a lot of "brotha's" in Mission, Texas.

John and Ana Davis. Aka, Shrek and the Princess.

John and Ana with Ana's mom. You are truly missed.

Mazatlán, Mexico Cruise. God is good all the time.

Nevertheless, I held my own. I honorably served eight (8) years in the United States Army and over twenty (20) years working for a local police department in Southern California. I was assigned to the Street Gang Unit when I met Ana.

Not to mention growing up in Southeast San Diego in a gang-populated area known for its gang shootings and narcotic activity. I was well aware of the different neighborhood communities plagued with gang rivalry and death.

I was not intimidated in any way. A chair was brought up, and I was asked to take a seat while this group of grown Texas men decided to inquire about who I was. The oldest asked me what my intentions were with their sister. Another asked if I had a job. I smiled and answered each question with the confidence I normally have when addressing anyone.

I was not cocky but direct with my answers. After this interview, it was clear I had passed the requirements needed to be accepted into the family. The final vote came from Ana's dear mom, who accepted me into the family from day one. I was blessed to be able to spend nine (9) more years with Ana's lovely mom.

It was hard on the family when Ana's mom passed away, but I believe in my heart this woman went directly to heaven because Ana's mom had a heart of gold. During those nine (9) years, I witnessed some of the best BBQ dishes being prepared right in front of my eyes. Ana's brother, Frank, would take me under his wing, show me the ropes and give me the basics of smoking a BBQ brisket, Texas-style. I would learn cooking a brisket was a very well-thought-out process.

John and Frank cooking BBQ outside.

This cooking process involves a lot of patience, time, mesquite wood, and Bud Light (Or actually any beer of your preference). I'm a Corona Premier man myself. Frank would always tell me he cooked his brisket with mesquite wood. I would ask Frank if he used any other wood when he cooked brisket. Frank said, "A true Texas man cooks brisket with mesquite."

John, Ana, Frank, and Melly spend time together in Miami, Florida (Fort Lauderdale Cruise). Yes, I'm wearing the same damn shirt I was wearing in the last photo. Hey, that Polo shirt was comfortable.

Frank would take another sip of beer and put more mesquite on the fire. I always loved watching Frank cook because Frank was cool, calm, and did not worry about the things I always worried about.

I would worry about the stall and wonder if the brisket would be done on time for guests arriving at the house. Frank explained to me that he had cooked so many briskets on so many occasions that it became natural for him to know when the brisket was done just by touching the exterior foil wrapped around it.

The force was definitely with Frank. Frank and I would continue to talk about brisket and sports. Frank made it clear to me from day one that he was a Dallas Cowboys fan for life. That was okay with me because everyone who knows anything about the NFL knows the Dallas Cowboys have always been "America's Team." I remember as a kid when we played football in the street, "Dead Man Sideline," whoever was quarterback was always Roger Staubach

I also made it clear to Frank that I was a Raiders fan for life. Frank just walked away and laughed. I walked away with Frank and tried to change the subject. It was years later, on Thanksgiving Day, when I would have the last laugh. To be exact, it was November 25th, 2021.

The Raiders, because Dak failed to score, beat the Cowboys 36-33. I love to cook brisket, and I love when the Raiders win football games. For several years now, I've just gotten better at cooking brisket. That's all I have for now.

Win, Lose, or Draw, Raiders for Life. Just Win. Please.

John and Ana taking a photo with California's favorite couple, Mickey and Minnie Mouse.

John and Ana… Raider Fans for Life.

God is good all the time. You just have to believe and have faith.

Hebrews 11:1 "Faith is confidence in what we hope for and assurance about what we do not see."

MY BARBECUE ADVENTURE

I've had a great life compared to others with similar backgrounds. I was adopted by loving parents who gave me the foundation to be where I am today. I met Ana during a very busy time in my life. I was a single parent raising a little girl, who I obtained custody of at the age of three (3).

Being in the police department did not give me a lot of time to be at home with my daughter, but I was financially able to take very good care of her. My daughter's mom took a path down to addiction, which destroyed our family. I was married for only two (2) years to a woman who enjoyed smoking crack more than taking care of her child/daughter.

The addiction period is a mother@#$%^#. I did what any person would do when you come to the realization you can do bad by yourself. I divorced this woman I was in love with and made a promise to myself that I would never subject myself or my daughter to such heartbreak again. I met Ana when my daughter was sixteen (16) years old.

I take my hat off to any single parent. I was a single parent for thirteen (13) years. I was the daddy, the mommy, the sister, and the brother. I prepared the meals, planned the babysitting schedule, attended the Girl Scout meetings, and did all the grocery and school shopping on my own. Not to mention the numerous hair appointments I attended, so my daughter's hair was the way she wanted it to be.

My poor daughter. In the beginning, all I could do was braid my daughter's hair into two (2) ponytails. The poor child went to school looking like "Pippi Longstocking." As the years went by, I got fancy and moved up to three (3) braids. Wow…

It became obvious my daughter would need to have her hair braided professionally throughout the year. The skills of cooking and preparing a meal, the skills my father taught me at an early age, definitely came in handy.

A responsible parent will "cook" meals at home when time permits. McDonalds, Jack in the Box, and Burger King, when I was growing up, were a treat. I was provided with three (3) square meals a day and numerous snacks throughout the day when I was growing up.

My dad would say I could eat whatever I wanted as long as I did not waste any food. I was blessed because I never went without, and neither did my daughter. You learn as your child or children grow that no matter what you do, no matter the sacrifices you make to better your child's life, your children will eventually make their own decisions in life in reference to what they decide to do.

Some children follow a productive path, and others, even when they are given the tools needed to succeed, take a different path down a non-productive trail leading to nothing successful. After a while, all you can do is pray for your child/children and hope they decide to make better choices in the future.

This is another story I will share at a later time. God willing. Ana was a traditional Hispanic woman who was married for twenty years (20) with three (3) boys. When I met Ana, she was working three (3) jobs. Ana had been divorced for over eight (8) years when we met.

Ana divorced her husband of twenty (20) years because of irreconcilable differences. My daughter, from day one, gave Ana a hard time when we met. Ana's two oldest boys, Mike and Rudy, were not very nice to me in the beginning. I don't blame the boys. The boys did not know me and what type of man I was.

I could just be passing through. I became very close to Ana's youngest child, Christopher. Christopher was going through a tough time when his parents divorced. Christopher was clearly angry over the divorce, as most kids normally are. I assured Christopher I was there to take care of his mother and to be a friend anytime he needed someone to talk to.

Christopher, throughout my relationship with his mother, has always been upfront and truthful with me. I'm very close to Christopher because, from day one, Christopher showed me he was a child with a beautiful, giving heart. By the grace of God, Ana and I were able to stay in a relationship that has lasted over sixteen (16) years.

Through prayers and time, I have earned the respect of all three (3) of Ana's boys. The boys know now that I'm a man of my word and I have done everything in my power to take care of their mom like the princess she is.

During my later years in the department, I started cooking for my fellow employees. I started cooking small dishes like chicken wings, macaroni and cheese, baked beans, and jalapeno poppers. On a few potlucks, I cooked/smoked a seven (7) bone prime rib.

The prime rib was definitely a hit. Captains, Lieutenants, and investigators from other units started showing up at our simple potlucks.

Seven (7) bone Prime Rib Roast.

I later graduated to smoking briskets and brought those briskets to work for the numerous potlucks we had throughout the year.

La Caja China Cooking Box.

My biggest gathering at my home consisted of sixty (60) guests. I purchased a Caja China Cooking Box, and I cooked a 100 lb. pig. Oh yeah. With the help of my Sergeant, Rick Castro, we took on this massive challenge. The cook was a success.

Piggy, piggy, piggy.

I asked my beloved friend, San Diego Police Detective Gary Phillips, how I was going to sit everyone comfortably in my small backyard. I was embarrassed because everyone was seated so close to each other just to make room.

My dear friend Gary, may he rest in peace, told me the following: "John, it does not matter. We're all together, and that is what is most important." Wise words from a beloved and missed friend. Thank you, Gary.

I began to see, after this successful gathering, how much joy was created around this cooking event. It was a pleasure to not only cook my first pig but also to see the joy on my guests' faces while they were eating the food that was prepared.

The pig was one of the main courses, but the potluck, in general, consisted of several various dishes, all made by loving hands. I wanted to create this feeling over and over again.

My wife was starting to complain about all the grills and smokers I had compiled in our small backyard. I didn't tell Ana I was looking forward to buying a Traeger Smoker next so I could challenge Frank again when he returned to California to visit.

I was able to calm my wife's nerves by promising to buy her a purse she had so badly wanted. I did not realize the purse she wanted was a $2,500 Louis Vuitton purse. I'm still walking funny after that purchase, and I never purchased any more grills.

I explained to my wife each grill/smoker I own has a particular purpose. I also explained to my beautiful wife that I noticed when I was cooking on any grill I decided to use, when it was time to eat, it was always quiet at the table.

All you could hear was, "Hmmm," "Wow, this is so tender," and "This tastes so good." I guess I succeeded in what I was trying to accomplish. When I retired, Ana and I decided to move out of California and move to Texas.

BBQ heaven, here I come. We moved to the Rio Grande Valley (R.G.V.), and I stayed retired for a few years before I became bored with staying home. Ana and I traveled a lot during my retirement years and enjoyed life as we should.

Ana and I went to some impressive BBQ restaurants in Texas during my retirement. We visited Franklin's BBQ in Austin, Texas, The Original Blacks BBQ in Lockhart, Texas (Mr. Black, the father, was still alive at that time), Terry Black's Barbecue in Austin, Texas, Cooper's Old Time Pit Bar B Que in New Braunfels, and the Ribshack Que in Fallbrook California just to name a few. When I say we ate. We ate.

Ana enjoying a beef rib bone at "The Ribshack Que" in Fallbrook, California.

John enjoying a beef rib at the Ribshack Que in Oceanside, California.

John and Ana eating BBQ at Ace's BBQ in Mission, Texas.

John eating at the Union Smokehouse BBQ, San Diego, California.

Terry Black's BBQ. Austin Texas.

Cooper's Old Time Pit Bar-B-Que.

Ana laughing after hearing John, aka "Wilbur," tell one of his silly jokes.
Happy wife. Happy Life.

I later decided I wanted to go back to work, but I wanted to do something fun and exciting. I really wanted to learn how to cook barbecue
in general but master the art of cooking barbecue brisket. Remember,

I was living in the RGV with Frank. There was no way I wasn't going to learn how to cook my brisket to perfection.

I watched numerous barbecue/brisket videos on the YouTube channel and purchased Franklin's Barbecue book called "A Meat-Smoking Manifesto" to gain more knowledge in the area of cooking barbecue brisket. I later decided to work at Rudy's "Country Store" and Bar-B-Que Restaurant.

LOVING IT AT RUDY'S BBQ RESTAURANT

My wife Ana thought I was crazy. Thirty-one (31) years in law enforcement, and I wanted to work at Rudy's "Country Store" and Bar-B-Q Restaurant. Yes, I did. I walked into Rudy's "Country Store" and Bar-B-Q Restaurant located in the City of Pharr. The General Manager identified himself as Taylor. This guy was cool as they came, and the environment inside the restaurant was friendly and inviting. Taylor looked at my resume and told me I was overqualified for the job. I explained to Taylor I had no experience in the BBQ restaurant business, but I was willing to learn. I was eager to start when I smelled the fragrance of smoked brisket.

As I talked to Taylor, I could actually feel his passion for BBQ. Taylor's smile lit up the room. I don't know why, but Taylor reminded me of Paul Newman in the movie, "Cool Hand Luke." Taylor's easy-going personality and the way he spoke to customers was just cool. Taylor made you feel right at home. Over the years, working in law enforcement, I have learned to read people very well by the mannerisms they display.

Taylor, aka "Cool Hand Luke." General Manager of Rudy's "Country Store" and Bar-B-Q in Pharr, Texas

Brisket Heaven.

Taylor had confidence, and I could tell he was a man of honor and integrity. I would find out later Taylor and I had a lot in common. Taylor showed me around the restaurant and introduced me to the head cook, Raul. Raul was what I would call an expert and professional when it came to cooking BBQ in general. Raul was an expert on the grill/smoker, and I'm proud to say Raul was my trainer. I was getting over twenty (20) years of BBQ experience from this man who was as humble as Christ.

John: Wearing my Rudy's "Country Store" and Bar-B-Q Restaurant work shirt.

Raul at Rudy's "Country Store" and Bar-B-Q Restaurant.

"Group Meals" provided by Rudy's "Country Store" and Bar-B-Q Restaurant. The prices displayed were the prices offered at the time of my employment. The listed prices for group meals may have changed over time.

Raul and I worked closely together, and I learned from the expert the types of wood you can use for brisket, the proper temperature at which you can cook it, and the correct resting times for brisket. Raul also showed me how to slice a brisket correctly.

I learned how to smoke briskets in the rain, cold, heat and any weather the RGV could dish out. Raul never missed a day of work, and neither did I. When Raul showed me the area where the briskets were being smoked, I was in brisket heaven.

The briskets looked like black gold to me. Hours and hours smoking and turning into this tender piece of meat that melted in your mouth. You have to remember if you dine at Rudy's up until 2 pm, you're eating food Raul prepared.

I learned about the whole restaurant system. I assisted in the dining area. I cooked and prepared everything on the menu. Rudy's even smokes prime rib on weekends. One of my duties was to load the smoker with numerous briskets. This task is not an easy job. A beef packer can weigh up to twelve (12) to eighteen (18) pounds. I will tell you from firsthand experience.

People who don't work in the barbecue industry do not realize the hard work that goes into making a great barbecue meal for others to eat. On the first day at work, Raul would show me how to open the oven doors safely so I would not get burned. I opened the oven door on numerous occasions throughout the day, and I will tell you, I felt like I was in the bowels of hell. I have burned my face, arms, and hands numerous times so I could properly cook the meat that was on the grill.

I'm not going to be the one that burns hundreds of dollars in products. "Not I," said Shrek." I prepared and cooked pork ribs, pork loin, baby back ribs, chicken, pork butts, pulled pork, turkey, and sausage on a daily basis. I'm not even talking about the side dishes. When I prepared the briskets, I was in brisket heaven.

Every time I prepared a brisket, I thought of my brother-in-law Frank. Is this right, Frank? I learned this, Frank. Frank, I think I can cook a brisket better than you. I would always try to make the best brisket I could. Of course, I would never cook a brisket as good as Frank. There were times Frank would touch the foil and tell me the brisket was not done.

I would ask Frank, where is your thermometer to check the meat? Frank would smile and tell me to get another beer. It was like I was the Jedi learning from the Master. After a week, I noticed Raul, Taylor, and other employees at the restaurant were constantly asking me if I liked my job. I was never late to work because I wanted to work at Rudy's "Country Store" and Bar-B-Q Restaurant.

I took pride in my job. I would tell Taylor, Raul, and anyone who would ask me on a daily basis that I loved my job and I had plans of staying for a while. The kitchen area is fast-paced. Working with the BBQ grill/smoker ovens is not a job for everyone.

Juvenile Corrections Officer John Davis at Evins Detention Facility.

I left Rudy's "Country Store" and Bar-B-Q Restaurant on great terms. I would advise anyone who loves barbecue and wants to know how to really prepare barbecue brisket and many other barbecue favorites for their family and friends to come and work at the restaurant. I left Rudy's due to a higher calling.

I was asked to work at a juvenile detention facility in the area that housed juvenile gang members from across the state of Texas. I had an opportunity to help some kids get their lives together. I wanted to be a positive role model for these kids who were labeled "gang members."

I wanted to share my story and explain to the kids that they had options and could do anything they put their minds to. My experience at Rudy's "Country Store" and Bar-B-Q Restaurant was life-changing.

I gained a better understanding of how to prepare barbecue brisket as well as other barbecue favorites by working at the restaurant. Rudy's "Country Store" and Bar-B-Q Restaurant are definitely places you need to take your family and friends. Excellent BBQ. Thank you, Taylor, Raul, Alexis, Victoria and the staff at Rudy's "Country Store" and Bar-B-Q Restaurant for the awesome experience.

Alexis and Victoria preparing a group platter of turkey and brisket for a customer.

WHAT IS BRISKET, AND WHERE DOES BRISKET COME FROM?

The brisket is the chest part of a steer. The chest part of a steer is muscular tissue, just like a bodybuilder's chest muscles. Like Arnold's rippling muscles. Think about all the weight a steer carries around. A steer is a neutered male bull calf. Now you know where brisket comes from. This is why the process of cooking a brisket can be time-consuming. The muscles in the chest area of the steer have to be cooked slowly so the tendons break down to give you tender meat. Done. Simple. Moving on.

Prime Packer Brisket from HEB.

Various Selections of Beef:

I'm a true believer the quality of meat you purchase has a lot to do with the end product. I cook for my dear friends and family members. I buy what I can afford. I also became great friends with my butcher. Always tip your butcher.

The U.S.D.A. (U.S. Department of Agriculture) grades their meat based on flavor, tenderness, and juiciness. The categories of meat are listed under Prime, Choice and Select.

Definition of Marbling: Simply put. Marbling is the fat strands found in beef. The more fat in the meat, the better the marbling. The fat can give you a better flavor, tenderness, and juiciness in the beef.

U.S.D.A. Prime Beef: Prime is the highest grade of meat with the most marbling/fat from the youngest steers. Prime beef is normally served in fancy restaurants or upscale steakhouses.

Prime is known for its tenderness, flavor, and all-around juiciness. You can never go wrong with a prime cut of meat. While prime meat is expensive, it's the best. Would you rather drive a Porsche or a Volkswagen? The engines in both cars are the same.

One engine has been upgraded, while the other engine is just the basic model. My first car was a Volkswagen Beetle. I loved that car, and that was what I could afford at the time.

U.S.D.A. Choice Beef: Choice beef is also considered a high-grade beef. The choice grade has less marbling/fat compared to the Prime grade of beef. Choice grade is what you normally find at your grocery store (Walmart, HEB, Vons, Ralphs, Costco, and Sam's Club). Most of the listed stores above also carry Prime Beef).

I live in Texas now, and I love HEB. HEB carries all cuts of beef. I have a brother-in-law who retired from HEB and explained to me that HEB means "Here Everything is Better." This is definitely a true statement. I have never gone wrong buying any type of meat from HEB.

To be honest with you, I have never gone wrong buying anything from HEB. HEB is the best. Yeeha. Of course, I do have a connection with my neighborhood butcher at Aguilar's Meat Market, located in the City of Mcallen, Texas, and I get the hook-up every time.

As I said before, don't forget to tip your butcher. It will pay off in the long run. I have cooked numerous briskets that were "Choice" grade beef. The brisket came out great each time. Choice grade beef is affordable for most budgets. Again, if I have the money, I'm going to my butcher for Prime. That's my opinion.

U.S.D.A. Select Beef: Select beef is a leaner cut of beef compared to Prime and Choice grade beef. Select has less marbling/fat. Due to the lower fat content, this cut of meat can have less juice and less flavor. Select beef is considered tender, but due to the meat having less marbling/fat, you may need to add additional flavor with seasoning or marinating.

Top (4) Four Cuts of Beef: The four (4) top cuts of meat, in my opinion, are Ribeye, Filet Mignon, New York Strip Loin and Porterhouse (A.K.A. as the T-Bone Steak).

These four (4) cuts of meat are considered the best based on tenderness and flavor. When I'm not cooking brisket, I'm cooking Ribeye Steaks, T-Bone Steaks, Cowboy Steaks, or Dino Beef Ribs.

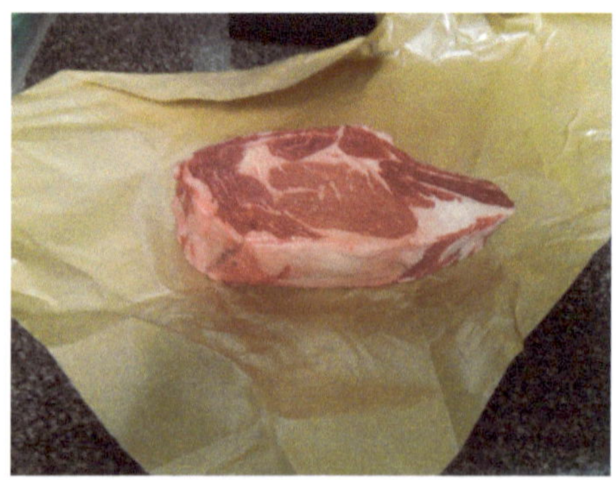

Prime Ribeye Steak

Tomahawk Ribeye Steak (Prime).

Dino Ribs (Prime).

Prime Ribeye Steaks. Yummy.

When I have dinner at a Brazilian Steakhouse, my wife will run up to the salad bar and fill up on salad, and the items I don't see are very appealing. Ana loves vegetables/her greens. I say yuck to veggies.

Sorry, but if I wanted to eat greens all day like a cow, I would eat my grass in the front yard for free. Everything at the steakhouse is top of the line. Ladies and Gentlemen, I'm a pure carnivore. I don't waste time eating the lower cuts of meat. When the "Gaucho" or waiter comes to the table, I select filet mignon with bacon or ribeye steak.

PREPARING AND SEASONING YOUR BRISKET

Tools needed:

1. Sharp "Flexible" Paring Knife or Silver skin Remover
2. Butcher Paper or Foil Paper
3. Large Cutting Board
4. Large Sheet Pan with Rack
5. Plastic Gloves
6. Ziploc Freezer Bags
7. Foil Deep Roasting Pan
8. Insulated Ice Chest with Towel
9. Your Favorite Beer or Alcoholic Beverage
10. A reliable Meat Thermometer
11. Music of your choice.
12. "Heat Proof Gloves" (Very Important To Have)

Ingredients:

1. Basic Texas Rub is Kosher Salt and Black Pepper
2. Morton's Kosher or Coarse Sea Salt

3. Pink Himalayan Salt
4. Brisket Pepper (Pepper from India)
5. Regular Black Pepper
6. 10 mesh Black Pepper.
7. Any favorite seasoning you like

Binding Agents for your Brisket:

There are numerous binding agents you can use to help your seasoning stick to your brisket. I have used olive oil and mustard on most occasions, but there are several other binding agents you can try. An independent bind, like mustard by itself, should not affect the taste of the meat.

Popular Binding Agents for Brisket:

1. Mustard
2. Mayonnaise (Mayo keeps moisture inside brisket)
3. Olive Oil
4. Apple Cider Vinegar
5. Beef Broth or Chicken Stock
6. Tomato Sauce
7. Barbecue Sauce
8. Worcestershire Sauce
9. Frank's favorite. Beer or Wine
10. Hot Sauce

You can also combine binders to create a new flavor. Duke says, "Give it a try." Ruff…

TRIMMING YOUR BRISKET

You have two (2) separate parts of a brisket. The Point and the Flat. Trim the fat on the brisket down to a 1/2 to 1/4 of an inch. Trim all silver skin off the brisket. This process will help more seasoning penetrate the meat but also give you a nice fat coat to protect the brisket during the smoking process.

I round the ends off the brisket down by the Point and Flat area. The Flat area of the brisket is the leaner cut of the brisket, which is attached to the lower breastbone. On this part of the brisket, I leave a thicker fat cap to protect the meat but remove enough fat so seasoning can penetrate this area of meat.

I personally keep more fat on the flat area because this area of the brisket doesn't have a lot of marbling and tends to dry out during the cook. The Point of the brisket is attached to the rib cage of the steer and has the most marbling/fat. I trim the fat cap down to 1/2 to 1/4 of an inch. I trim off all brown areas around the brisket.

The easiest way to trim a brisket if you're short on time is to have your butcher trim the brisket. Purchase your brisket, and then kindly ask the butcher to trim the fat cap on your brisket down to 1/2 to 1/4 inch. It saves you time

, and you can have your butcher save excess fat for another cook. I personally like trimming my brisket myself.

Trimming off excess fat will speed up the cooking time and bring the full flavor potential out of the brisket. More seasoning can also penetrate your meat. There is a large pocket of fat that connects the Point and the Flat on the brisket. This area is called the deckle.

This is the area where you will see a thick layer of fat that attaches the Point and the Flat together. This area contains hard chunks of fat that will need to be trimmed down/removed. This area of fat will not be rendered off during cooking.

This part of the brisket looks like a large block of solid cheese. This area will need to be trimmed down so seasoning can be added to it. I don't trim all the fat from this area of the brisket. I keep some of the fat in this area because it will keep the Point areas of the brisket moist and juicy.

The amount of fat you take off this area is totally up to you. Remember to trim all the dark pieces of meat off your brisket.

You want your brisket to be rounded and even in shape to expose more areas of the brisket to the smoke and to cook your brisket evenly through the cooking process.

My brother-in-law Frank takes his brisket from the bag and rinses his brisket off with water. I have watched Frank season a brisket right out of the bag and onto the smoker. Frank doesn't trim anything off his brisket. Every brisket this man has smoked is a masterpiece. No special seasonings.

A traditional Texas-style brisket is only kosher salt and black pepper. Of course, every question I had for Frank, no matter what the question was, involved an answer followed by a drink of Bud Light. I have watched numerous videos on how to properly trim your brisket. I also learned trimming your brisket helps the brisket absorb the smoke better once inside the smoker.

Before I worked for Rudy's "Country Store" and Bar-B-Q, I would watch YouTube videos to learn how to properly season/smoke and slice a brisket. There are hundreds of great videos you can watch to learn how to trim/slice a brisket correctly.

I have several go-to videos I watched when I first started out on this quest to learn more about brisket. A good friend of mine, Greg Mrvich, started his YouTube channel called "Ballistic BBQ" before I retired.

Watching Greg's BBQ videos inspired me to learn more about cooking brisket and other barbecue dishes as well. I watched these various videos Greg would produce so I would be able to make a better brisket than Frank:).

Can I make a better brisket than Frank? Well, to be honest with you, I don't need to make a better brisket than Frank. Frank is my brother-in-law, and I love the man to death. I have no problems sitting back and eating Frank's impressive BBQ brisket during a family gathering. That way, I can relax and sit back and drink my beer.

The list of YouTube video websites I have listed below definitely increased my knowledge on my road to cooking the perfect Texas-style barbecue brisket. Ballistic BBQ, Meat Church BBQ, Smoke Master D, and Mad Scientist BBQ, just to name a few. When I moved to Texas, I also started watching Arnie Tex's YouTube videos on the YouTube Channel.

I will go into detail in a later chapter on how to slice your brisket correctly after it has rested. In time, you will find a trimming method that works best for you. When it comes to seasonings/rubs, I have my personal favorites. I have listed a few of my favorite rubs for your review.

Go out there and try every rub you can so you can find the flavor you and your family are looking for. I really did not get into different brisket rubs until I came to Texas, so most of the brisket rubs I use now are Texas-based brands. Here are a few brisket rubs I think you will like. I have listed the rubs in no particular order or preference. Each rub brings its own flavor.

1. Rudy's Rub
2. 2 Gringo's Chupacabra Rub Brisket Magic
3. 2 Gringo's Chupacabra Rub All Seasoning Meat Rub
4. Fiesta Brand Extra Fancy Brisket Rub
5. TXQ Rubs 956
6. Franklin Spice Rubs
7. Salt Lick Original Dry Rub
8. Terry Black's Barbecue Beef Dry Rub
9. Kosmos Dry Rubs

10. True Texas BBQ Salt and Pepper Blend
11. Surf and Turf Spanglish Asadero

Ratio:

½ teaspoon of kosher salt for one pound of meat. 50/50 or remember 1 Tablespoon is equal to three (3) teaspoons. It all depends on taste. You can also add garlic powder, onion powder or any other seasoning you would like to use.

I have learned the bark for my brisket comes out better when I use plain old kosher salt and black pepper. There are endless products out there you can use to take out the guesswork on what type of flavor you would like to produce on your brisket.

Oh, I almost forgot. I have the perfect apple cider turkey brine recipe for you. You definitely need to try this recipe. Ana and I came down during the Thanksgiving season to spend time with Ana's mom. There was a small family gathering, and I was asked if I could cook the turkey.

I felt honored when I was asked to cook the main dish for Thanksgiving dinner. At the same time, I was not at home and would not be able to use the smoker I normally cooked on. That was a huge disadvantage to me, but I learned when you know what you're doing, it doesn't matter what you cook. You just get it done.

I thought to myself, I must make this turkey the best turkey anyone has ever had. I did not want to smoke the turkey because I was told another guest was bringing a smoked turkey. I was definitely put on the spot. Then, an idea came to me.

I watched a YouTube video by the BBQ Pit Boys one Thanksgiving that gave you step-by-step instructions on how to make this impressive brine. This recipe by the BBQ Pit Boys would save the day. I ended up going to the nearest HEB and grabbing all the ingredients for this apple cider brine. I then went to Home Depot to grab a 5-gallon plastic container to let the turkey marinate in.

Ana's mom watched me prepare this brine. **(I will attach a photo of the brine I made one Thanksgiving dinner when Ana and I were home for your review).** My only problem was I was unable to let the turkey sit in the brine overnight. I had about ten (10) hours to have this turkey ready for dinner.

The turkey marinated in the apple cider brine for 4-6 hours. I ended up cooking the turkey in the oven because I did not think the turkey would be done by the time the guest arrived if I cooked the turkey outside on the backyard grill.

I cooked the turkey in the oven at a higher temperature than recommended in the video provided by the BBQ Pit Boys. I crossed my fingers because this was not the time to blow it. The main course was on me, and Ana's mom was watching me.

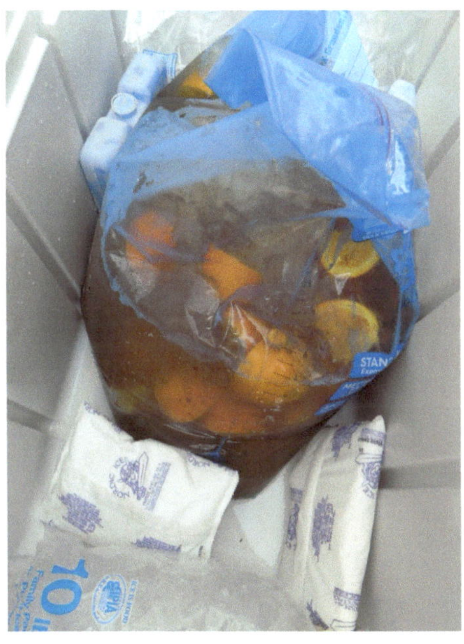

Apple Cider Brine Recipe by the BBQ Pit Boys.

Apple Cider Brine Recipe by the BBQ Pit Boys.

Apple Cider Brine Turkey on my Titan Stainless Rotisserie Grill.

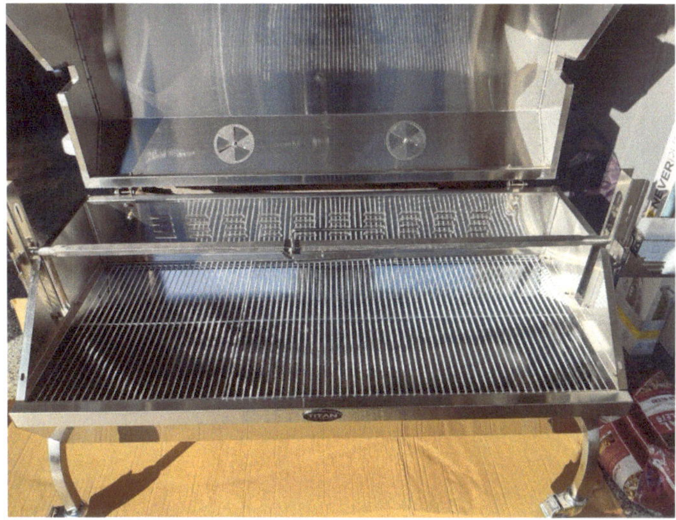

The Titan Stainless Steel Grill with Rotisserie attachment. Oh yeah, now we're cooking…

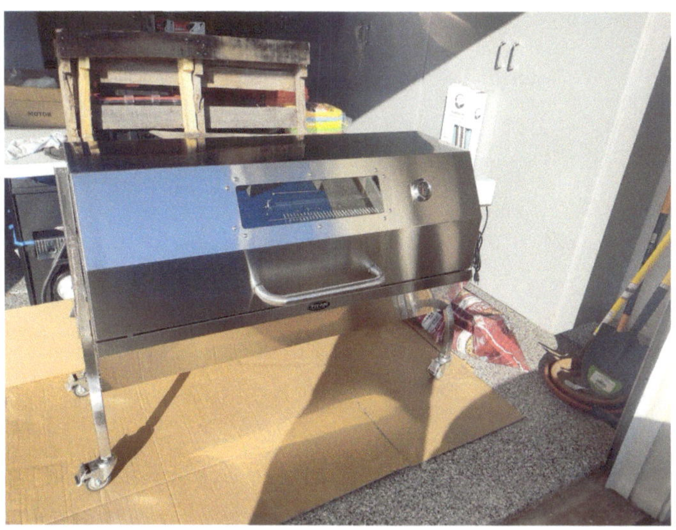

Titan Stainless Rotisserie Grill.

Ana's mom only spoke Spanish, so I used my Spanish Translator to communicate with Mom. I know, I know. I should be able to speak "Spanish." I took "Spanish" in high school, so I can understand what people are saying most of the time. A few of Ana's brothers taught me "Spanish." I can't repeat the "Spanish" I learned from the brothers in this book. The guest bringing his turkey arrived and placed his turkey on the table.

The turkey was wrapped in foil, but you could see the skin on the turkey looked flawless. I was still waiting for my turkey to finish cooking. By the time my turkey was finished, the family was just sitting down at the table to eat. I placed the apple cider brine turkey right next to the turkey brought to the house by the guest.

I have to admit my turkey presentation looked great. We started dinner and I waited to see what everyone's response would be. Ana started making my plate and whispered in my ear, "I love you, babe." Your turkey is going to be great, as always. My wife's encouragement meant a lot to me. Everyone started to eat, and it was quiet. I took a bite of the turkey the guest brought to the house.

The color of the skin was perfect, but when I took a bite of the turkey's white meat, it was so dry. Everyone who tasted my turkey said my turkey was excellent, and they wanted to know how I prepared the bird. I was going to tell them the recipe when Ana's mom asked to be taken to the kitchen for a minute. I got up from the table, and Ana and I walked Ana's mom to the kitchen to see what was wrong.

Ana's Mom started talking to Ana in "Spanish." I was unable to understand what Ana's mom was saying. Ana smiled, and told me her mother said, "No le digas a nadie la receta, es nuestro secreto." "La receta es de nuestra exclusiva propiedad." English Translation: "Don't tell anyone the recipe." The recipe is our secret, and it belongs to us only.

I laughed and said, "Yes, Mom." "The secret will be ours only." I must say that particular Thanksgiving dinner was the most memorable because, at the time, we did not know Mom would only be able to share Thanksgiving with her family for a few more years.

A shout-out to the BBQ Pit Boys. Thank you for making such great meals/YouTube videos for everyone to enjoy. PS: I love your videos. You guys remind me of ZZ Top.

TIME TO LET YOUR SEASONING PENETRATE YOUR BRISKET

I like to season my brisket and place the brisket onto a large sheet pan with a wire rack. I place the brisket into the fridge uncovered. This is the time I let the seasoning, mainly the kosher salt, penetrate the meat. I want the kosher salt to draw the moisture out of the brisket.

Once the kosher salt has done its job, I let the meat stay in the fridge overnight so the moisture that was drawn out settles back into the meat. I guess you can say the meat is being brined or tenderized during this process. The process, in general, is called osmosis.

I let my brisket sit in the fridge for a minimum of six (6) hours or overnight. The longer you let your seasoning sit on your brisket, the more the seasoning penetrates the meat. This process will create a flavorful and juicy brisket. A twelve (12) hour wait in the fridge is excellent if you have the time. I have also wrapped my brisket in butcher paper and plastic wrap overnight. No matter what method you would like to use, the process of drawing moisture out of the meat will be the same.

John's Man Cave Fridge. I had to remove the beer so I would have room for my meat.

When I'm cooking for family or friends, I don't over-season my meat. Everyone's salt intake is different. You can definitely use a large amount of salt on a brisket due to the portion of meat being so dense.

Most experts will say you can use a large amount of salt, and your brisket will be fine. This is a true statement because the meat in question is very dense. I have high blood pressure, which is controlled by medication. I know the dangers of hypertension and how salt can negatively affect your overall health.

With that said, I use enough salt to give my meat a subtle flavor. I let my guests and loved ones determine how much salt they would like on their cut of meat.

WHAT KIND OF SMOKER SHOULD I BUY?

I could write a book on this subject alone. I wish when I started seriously thinking about smoking BBQ, I would have had a manual on what to buy. I wasted a lot of time and money on inferior grills/smokers, which in time would need to be replaced.

I would buy these cheap smokers/grills that were really only made for hamburgers, hot dogs, and ribeye steaks from time to time. Whatever grill/smoker you intend to buy, definitely learn how to clean the smoker/grill. Take your time and compare smokers/grills. I can say, by trial and error, what smoker/grill you should buy. I'm no expert, and again, this is only my opinion as a common Joe.

When I first started smoking brisket, the Weber Smokey Mountain was a top choice for beginning grillers/smokers. Unfortunately, I did not want to spend the money and did not do any research on smokers or grills. I purchased the cheap stuff without realizing months/years later that I would need to upgrade.

The Weber Smokey Mountain Cooker/Smoker 14" is by far a perfect grill/smoker to buy if you're just starting out. If you're willing to spend a little more, you can bump up to the Weber Smokey Mountain Cooker/Smoker 18".

This cooker, a 14" model, is an all-in-one cooker that will cost you $279 and won't break your bank. This cooker has superior heat retention, which is important when cooking brisket. When cooking it, you must have a smoker that can retain a constant temperature during your cook.

Your fuel source is charcoal, and you have precise heat controls with adjusting dampers. You can use wood chips to create that smoky aroma for your food. I learned you can put wood chips inside foil and poke holes in the foil. Put the wood chips over your heat source, and the wood chips burn slowly and effectively.

You can also soak your wood chips in water or use the wood chips dry. Either way, you will get the desired smokey effect, and the wood chips flavors are versatile. I should have started with this smoker/cooker. I did not. I wasted money. Before you start cooking, do your research. Don't buy something cheap. Buy something dependable.

I now have eight (8) various grills/smokers in my BBQ arsenal. All my grills do something different and cook in various ways. As I made more money throughout my law enforcement career, I was able to buy more expensive but durable smokers/grills.

The smokers/grills I have purchased have been proven to be reliable. I have not needed to replace a smoker/grill to this day. My smokers/grills have lasted me for years because I take care of them.

The Pit Barrel Cooker/Smoker is another awesome smoker/grill to have in your arsenal. This smoker has produced the best chicken I have ever cooked. This smoker (22.5") has numerous videos on YouTube you can watch. The inventor of this smoker demonstrates how to use his smoker on his YouTube videos. Awesome idea. This inventor is the man...

The Pit Barrel Smoker/Grill 22.5"

I really became a Pit Barrel user for life when the inventor of this smoker showed owners of his product how to use his smoker/grill. Again, the price of $399 (18.5" Classic Pit Barrel) is excellent based on what you're getting with this product.

This smoker/cooker also uses a charcoal fuel source. I have also used lump charcoal with a mixture of charcoal briquettes as a fuel source. The good thing about Weber Smokey Mountain and the Pit Barrel Smoker is that the cost stays the same no matter where you buy the product—no surprise cost to own these excellent smokers/grills.

The Big Green Egg is another exceptional grill/smoker/oven.

You can not only make an awesome brisket in the Big Green Egg, but you can also bake pizza on the heating stone that comes with this oven. The Big Green Egg is your outdoor oven for any dish you would like to create for your family. The Big Green Egg The only thing I did not like about the Big Green Egg had nothing to do with its cooking ability.

Ana and I were blessed to buy a house, so we had to move out of the apartment we were staying in. That Big Green Egg was a mother to move. It was heavy as @#$%.

Being the macho man I thought I was, I believed I could move this smoker on my own. It has a stand with wheels, so I thought I would not have to carry the smoker far. Wrong Shrek. Wrong. I picked this smoker up and carried it twenty (20) feet before I had to put it down. I almost crapped on myself and did not have my Depends on that day.

All kidding aside, that smoker was dead weight. Unfortunately, the Big Green Egg fell over during the move. When I opened the lid, the internal clay fire bowl cracked. I was pissed. The exterior of the Big Green Egg was fine. I later ordered a new interior clay fire bowl, and I was up and running again.

I actually learned how to smoke brisket old school by using an Oklahoma Joe Longhorn Offset Smoker. When I purchased this smoker, I was ready for the big-league cooks. This smoker is my baby because it's so dependable. 751 square inches in primary cooking space. 300 square inches of secondary cooking space.

The fuel source is hardwood split chunks of any wood you would like to use as a fuel source. You can also use charcoal, lump charcoal, or charcoal briquette as a fuel source. I was able to get the Oklahoma Joe Longhorn Offset Smoker/Grill after Frank visited me in California one Summer.

Frank came down to visit one Summer and wanted to cook a brisket. Of course, this was my chance to watch the pro at work. I let Frank use this old cheap grill I had purchased mainly for hot dogs and burgers. Frank finished his brisket and continued to chuck mesquite wood into my cheap smoker.

I asked Frank why he was still putting wood into the smoker box because the brisket was already cooked. Frank would tell me he just loved the scent of mesquite. Frank held the temperature of that grill/smoker to 500 plus degrees, and we weren't cooking anything. The grill began to warp, and the temperature gauge cracked due to the intense heat the mesquite wood was producing.

My neighbors came to the house wondering what I was cooking because of the distinct aroma of mesquite in the air. After this embarrassing incident, I was able to get my Oklahoma Joe Longhorn Offset Smoker.

I never had a smoker warp on me ever again. I have had my Oklahoma Joe Longhorn Offset Smoker for well over ten (10) years. The smoker was well worth the $500 bucks that Ana spent to get me this smoker. Yes, Ana purchased this smoker for me. I deserved to be spoiled, too.

EASY BAKE OVEN OF SMOKERS/GRILLS

The Pit Boss Grill/Smoker is one of the easiest smokers I have ever worked with. You literally set your temperature and walk away. The smoker comes with an app that can be monitored and programmed from your phone. This excellent smoker takes the guesswork out of your cook.

I purchased a Pit Boss Smoker, and I have been extremely happy with the smoker's performance. During rain, cold weather, and extreme weather conditions, this smoker continues to perform. What I like most about this grill is its versatility when it comes to the variety of wood pellets you can use.

You can use mesquite, cherry, apple, peach, hickory, maple, or any fruit wood pellet you can find to put in your hopper. The combination of various wood pellets is endless. A full wood pellet hopper on a Pit Boss can cook for ten (10) or more hours. I know this because I have cooked brisket for 10-12 hours, and the smoker maintained the heat throughout my cooking.

Most of my cooks were performed on a Pit Boss Smoker/Grill, as you can see from the photographs I have provided for your review. Another pellet grill on the market is called the Traeger Wood Pellet Grill/Smoker.

The Traeger Smoker is another exceptional smoker you should consider adding to your BBQ arsenal. I don't own a Traeger, but I have had the pleasure of cooking on a Traeger, and I was very pleased with the performance.

The Traeger is more expensive in price but well worth it if you can fork out the dollars. I have attached a comparison link discussing the differences between the Traeger Smoker and the Pit Boss Smoker. You can decide for yourself. No matter what you decide to buy, I guarantee you will be happy with your purchase.

https://www.msn.com/en-us/lifestyle/shopping/pit-boss-vs-traeger-who-makes-the-better-pellet-grill/ar-AA1qsD3m?ocid=msedgdhp&pc=U531&cvid=0b7074ac14134ded9099111e0b42d7ca&ei=13

KEEP YOUR SMOKER/GRILL CLEAN

I would say that with any smoker or grill, you have to maintain the cooker. This means you have to keep the smoker clean. I will say that again: Please keep your smoker clean. I had a neighbor in California who seemed to always come outside when I was cooking or smoking something. The neighbor never took care of his yard.

By the time I had purchased the home next door to this neighbor, the vines coming from his side of the fence had consumed the fence separating our properties. My exterminator stated the vines were attracting mice, roof rats, possums and ants, which lived throughout this invasive plant. The vine had taken the fence over, so when I purchased the property, the weight of the vine was destroying the integrity of the fence and the fence line.

Of course, this neighbor did nothing. I took matters into my own hands and called a landscape company to cut the vines off my side of the fence. I then sprayed the vines so the vines would not continue to grow on my side of the fence. Problem solved. This eyesore was gone, but I did not realize that by removing the vines, this neighbor could now look through the fence and gaze into my yard. I really did not think anything about it at the time.

Ana stated that every time she went outside, this neighbor would come outside and start to whistle. Why, Lord, do I have to deal with the creepy and weird? My wife is very attractive, so I believed this guy was trying to get some extra looks at my beautiful wife. Being the Shrek I was, I was going to start watching this guy more closely. Ana went outside one morning to do some gardening like she normally did.

I stood by the upstairs bedroom window to see if "Mr. Whistles" would come out of his burrow to investigate. Like clockwork, "Mr. Whistles" appears. I watched this guy glaring through the fence at Ana. I yelled, "Good morning, Sir." "How are you doing today?" Mr. Whistles strangely retreated back into his house. Hmm. I wonder why?

One day, when I was outside smoking this beautiful brisket, "Mr. Whistles" was outside, apparently trying to cook something on his grill. I was on the opposite side of the fence smoking a brisket I had started at 12 am that morning.

I looked over and saw flames coming from my neighbor's grill that were reaching the second story of his home. Not to mention, these possible flames could endanger my home, which was next door. The guy was trying to put a grease fire out with his water hose. It was clear the fire was getting out of control.

I grabbed the fire extinguisher I kept outside and handed the fire extinguisher to "Mr. Whistles." The guy had no clue how to use the fire extinguisher. I quickly gave "Mr. Whistles" instructions on how to use the fire extinguisher. "Mr. Whistles" was able to successfully control the fire and eventually put the fire out. Unfortunately, "Mr. Whistles" burned a small portion of his balcony.

I waited a few weeks, thinking this neighbor would replace my fire extinguisher, which I let him borrow/use. "Mr. Whistles" never replaced my fire extinguisher. The lesson learned is to be prepared to control a fire anywhere in your home.

Educate yourself on how to use a fire extinguisher and keep your grill/smoker clean to prevent grease fires. Your insurance company and neighbors will appreciate your preparedness. When I clean my grill/smoker, I use a product I purchased from Home Depot called Citrusafe. Yes, I have also worked at Home Depot. The Home Depot in Mission, Texas, in my opinion, is hands down the best Home Depot Store in the R.G.V. Awesome store.

Home Depot. "How Doers Get More Done!"

I clean my grill grates and the bottom of my grill where the grease can settle periodically. I do like to keep some oils already embedded in the grill/smoker's interior to a minimum. These oils keep the grill/smoker "seasoned," which can add flavor to the meats being cooked.

After cleaning the grill grates, I coat the grates with olive oil to keep the grill/smoker "seasoned" and to prevent the grates from rusting. Cleaning your grill on a regular basis, depending on how much you cook, will keep it in tip-top condition and prevent grease fires from occurring.

COOKING TIME FOR YOUR BRISKET

Well, well, well. The moment of truth. This is one of the many questions always asked when cooking a brisket. What temperature should I smoke my brisket at? How long will it take to cook my brisket? Do I wrap my brisket or keep my brisket unwrapped? I will do my best to answer these many questions based on my own trial and error when cooking brisket. Anytime you smoke a brisket, the temperature of the smoker should be able to hold a consistent temperature of 250 degrees.

This is basic. Yes, you can cook a brisket at a lower temperature of 225 degrees, but why would you? The lower the temperature, the longer it will take to finish your dinner. I learned this in my early days with my brother-in-law, Frank. If you're looking, you're not cooking. "Teddy Allen" originally came up with that famous barbecue quote, if you're wondering. Please, please, please. Let your brisket cook. You will be tempted to open the lid to see if your bark is forming. It's okay to open the lid to check on your brisket after a few hours have passed.

If you tend to check on your brisket every dang hour, you're going to be adding unnecessary cooking time to your cook. Not to mention extending your "stall" time. Once your smoker has a temperature of 250 degrees, keep the dang lid closed. The brisket will need to hit an internal temperature of 160 degrees. The time it takes to reach 160 degrees internally is called the stall stage. The stall stage can take hours to overcome. Of course, if you raise the temperature, you will clear the stall stage faster.

There is a technique called the "Texas Crutch" Frank showed me. When you hit the internal temperature of 160 degrees, you wrap the brisket with foil. I prefer butcher paper. Wrapping the brisket in foil will cause the brisket to cook faster because the meat is being insulated by the foil.

I have learned that wrapping your brisket in foil can also cause the brisket to be in a steam environment, causing the bark on the brisket to be soft and mushy. You can overcome this by unwrapping the brisket during your final hours of cooking and letting the steam be released from the foil container/wrapping.

I like to smoke my brisket until I get a nice bark on the outer layer of the brisket. I check my brisket every few hours to see the outer appearance of the brisket. I'm checking to see if the bark on the brisket is forming. I have cooked my brisket uncovered the entire cook, and I have also cooked my brisket covered once I hit the stalling temperature of 160 degrees.

It all depended on the exterior look of my brisket. If my bark was the right color, I would wrap my brisket. If my bark had not formed, I kept cooking and left my brisket uncovered. A consistent temperature is key. This is why pellet grills/smokers make cooking brisket simple. Most smokers have an app you can use while you're cooking.

You set the temperature of the smoker and the internal temperature of your brisket. The smoker does the rest. The smoker will notify you when you have reached the desired temperature you are looking for.

Depending on who you talk to or ask, you normally pull your brisket at 203 degrees.

This is a general rule, but again, it all depends on the cut of meat and the tenderness of the meat when it reaches 203 degrees. When you pull any meat off the grill, it is still cooking internally. That's ribeye steak, chicken, ribs, any meat, period. With that said, if you pull your brisket at 201 degrees, the internal temperature may rise to 205 degrees.

On one occasion, I fell asleep while cooking a brisket, and when I woke up, my brisket was at a staggering internal temperature of 210 degrees. I was not using a pellet grill during this particular cook. I was using my old faithful Oklahoma Joe Offset Smoker. I was truly upset because I believed the brisket was ruined.

The brisket I was preparing was for a cookout/potluck scheduled to take place in about 6-8 hours. Surprisingly, that brisket, which I thought I had overcooked, came out very tender and juicy. That particular brisket was a prime cut of meat, and I believe the excessive marbling saved the day.

Don't panic if you can't exceed an internal temperature of 160 degrees for hours. If you panic, and I have before, you will adjust the temperature, open the lid to peek, and do all kinds of things you should not do.

Grab a beer like Frank and just wait. The internal temperature of 160 will break, and you will be on your way to having an awesome brisket. Always be familiar with your grill/smoker. Be familiar with the cut of meat you will be cooking. Be aware of the weight and size of your brisket after you trim the fat from your brisket.

Have an estimated time when you think your brisket will be completed. Start your cooking early. The larger the brisket, the longer the cook. Cooking/Smoking time for brisket is normally 1 ½ hours smoking time per pound of meat.

Remember, you got this. Relax and take a deep breath. Your brisket will come out fine. Trust me. Kiss your wife and kids. If you don't have a wife or kids, kiss your dog, cat, parrot, hamster, snake, turtle etc, etc. You get the point. All will be well.

RESTING YOUR BRISKET

This chapter is the most important part of my book. Resting your brisket is vital for a juicy and tender brisket. When you pull your brisket off the smoker, you will need to let the brisket rest. In major restaurants, a device called a proofer holds the brisket at a certain temperature for hours so the juices in the meat can settle.

The holding temperature in a proofer has to be above 140 to 160 degrees. If you don't have a proofer, you can use an insulated ice chest and a towel. Monitor your internal temperature with a meat thermometer.

When you pull your brisket, you should have an internal temperature between 201 and 205 degrees. Wrap your brisket and place your brisket inside a cooler. Place a meat probe inside the brisket to monitor its internal temperature. The temperature will rise five (5) to ten (10) degrees. This is normal.

The temperature will then begin to drop slowly. Depending on when your guests will arrive, it will determine when you pull your brisket for slicing. I rest my brisket between two (2) and three (3) hours. I have also rested my brisket for longer. The perfect carving temperature for brisket is between 195 and 205 degrees. Make sure you have a foil pan available to serve your brisket in. You need a deep foil pain so you can capture the juices during carving.

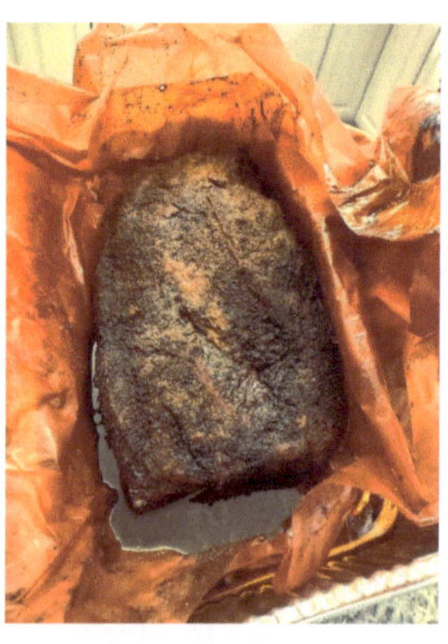

SLICING YOUR BRISKET THE EASY WAY

Well, we have reached that time where it is time to serve your brisket to your guests/loved ones. I will make this very simple. As I explained in my earlier chapters, brisket is made up of two (2) major muscle groups: the Point and the Flat.

When you unwrap your brisket, it will be very moist and dripping with juices you captured in your foil or butcher paper wrap. The fat drippings from the brisket can be captured in your foil deep roasting pan. I pour all the fat drippings into the foil pan.

I use these juices to baste my brisket slices to keep the brisket moist and juicy prior to serving my guests. If your brisket has plenty of marbling or you baste your brisket with Wagyu beef tallow, your brisket is certain to be extremely tender and juicy. I basted my brisket with Wagyu beef tallow, and the results were excellent.

The brisket was tender and juicy, with a shiny appearance that covered the entire bark of the brisket. The Wagyu beef tallow really made the bark of the brisket sparkle/shine. You can separate the two (2) muscles by cutting in between the Point and the Flat. This area of the brisket is connected by a huge piece of fat I identified earlier as the "large pocket of fat that binds the Flat and the Point on the brisket."

When you unwrap your brisket, it will be very moist and dripping with juices you captured in your foil or butcher paper wrap. This will be the fat that is rendered down during the cooking/smoking process. Separate the Point and the Flat with a sharp knife. Grab the Flat portion of the brisket and cut the brisket into thin slices.

A good representation of a thin slice of brisket would be the size of a pen or your index finger. Imagine your index finger split down the middle. That would be an average slice of brisket. If your brisket has plenty of marbling/fat, it won't matter how thick or thin you cut your brisket slices. Each slice will still be tender and juicy.

Slice the Flat portion of the brisket thinly across the grain of the meat approximately 1/2 inch in diameter. Look for the muscle fibers in the meat. You want to cut against the natural direction of the fibers in the meat.

Make sure you use a reliable, sharp knife to cut your brisket slices. "Burnt ends" are made from the portions of meat coming from the Point side of the brisket.

Ana likes slices from the fatter part of the brisket, the Point. I grab the Point and turn the Point approximately 90 degrees (A perfect "L" shape).

Once you have turned the Point 90 degrees, you can start slicing it starting at the end of the Point. You can also slice the Point down the middle to make your Point slices smaller in length. Slice accordingly and serve.

If you're like me, I learn by visually looking at something. Mad Scientist BBQ, on YouTube, has a step-by-step video I found very helpful when I was starting out learning the basics of barbecue brisket.

All the YouTube videos I shared with you are the way I was able to get more and more into mastering the art of cooking a brisket. I thank all those expert BBQ masters for all the information they share. Those videos helped me, and they can help you. Don't be afraid to try a new recipe or cooking style.

This is how you get better at cooking. I watched these Masters of BBQ perform so I could give that same magic and love to my family and friends. I became rich by seeing my family and friends happy when I cooked a meal they all enjoyed. That's all I really wanted to do.

I FINALLY MADE IT TO FRANKLIN'S BARBECUE

Ana and I were finally on our way to Austin, Texas. I have always wanted to try Franklin's BBQ for years, and now I had my chance. T.S.A. (Transportation Security Administration) finally reached out to me. I had a scheduled interview in Austin, Texas, and was excited about this new job opportunity.

I have always wanted to help people in any way I could. I also have personal reasons for wanting to work for T.S.A. (God willing, I will talk further about my need to work for T.S.A. in my next book. If there is even a next book.)

Ana and I drove up a day before my interview because I wanted to be familiar with the area. I hate being late for anything. I also wanted to definitely drive by Franklin's BBQ Restaurant. This was a big deal for me. Ana smiled because Ana knew this experience would be the icing on my cake.

The business was closed, and I stood outside just looking at this iconic BBQ location. I had an interview the following day, and I was not going to be in Austin for long. As I stood there looking like I was some transient thinking about breaking into the place, a car drove up, and a female exited the car.

I walked up to the lady and advised that I was originally from San Diego, California, and my wife Ana and I really wanted to know what was the best time to come have BBQ at the restaurant. The lady explained to me the best time to come was most likely during the week.

The lady stated the weekends were pretty busy. I had already done my research and learned you sometimes have to camp out the night before just to get into the restaurant. I thanked the lady for her time and walked away with my head hanging down. My interview was scheduled for the next day, and I knew by the time I left my interview with T.S.A. that my chances of getting into Franklin's BBQ were slim to none.

Ana and I went back to our hotel, and the whole night I imagined I made it inside Franklin's BBQ Restaurant. I was laughing with Ana and eating the best BBQ I could ever imagine. Then I woke up and realized this would be the closest I would ever come to going to Franklin's BBQ.

The next morning, I got up and prepared for my interview. Ana and I went downstairs to eat, and I asked every person I saw if they experienced the mouthwatering brisket at Franklin's BBQ. I was surprised that a lot of people told me they would rather go to another BBQ restaurant than stand in line for hours to get brisket from Franklin's BBQ.

I was floored because I would stand outside for hours to try Franklin's BBQ. I'm sorry, Lord, but I thought these people were just plain stupid. Forgive me, Lord, but that is how I truly felt. What is wrong with these people? I drove over to my interview, and after my interview, I was told I had the job. I was so happy I got the job.

I then drove over to Franklin's BBQ to say goodbye and take some photographs of the outside of the building. Ana and I drove up, and I could not believe my eyes. There was a short line, and Franklin's was scheduled to open in a few hours.

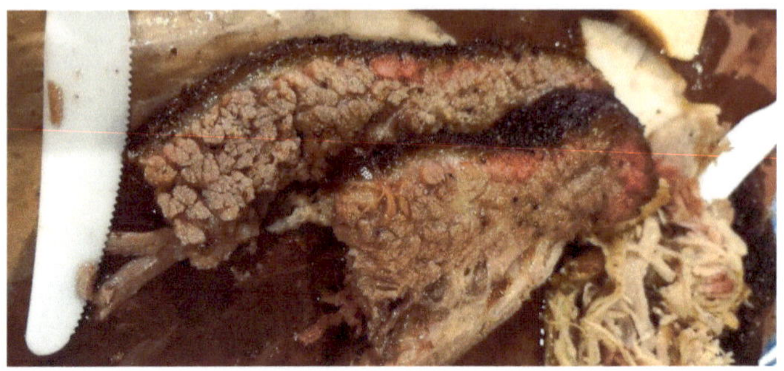

Franklin's BBQ Brisket Slices.

Ana and I ran to the line. Well, I ran to the line, leaving Ana to lock the car doors—sorry, babe. We were officially in line. A lady came out and took our order, and all I could say was, Brisket, Brisket. We walked up to the counter to order and ordered everything. The guy cutting the brisket reached into the proofer and pulled a fresh brisket out that was still wrapped in butcher paper.

The juices were pouring off this brisket like water. The cutter unwrapped the brisket, and this brisket looked amazing. The meat was actually glistening as the brisket was laid onto the cutting board. The cutter sliced the brisket and laid the slices down on the plate. I took a picture of the meal we were about to eat.

I was so ready to try this brisket that I took a picture of the platter and cut Ana's head off in the picture by mistake. I was only concerned about the brisket I had waited so long to enjoy. I put a slice of brisket into my mouth, and I could feel the brisket breaking down inside my mouth before I could even chew the meat.

The meat was effortless to chew. This piece of brisket I had in my mouth was the best brisket I have ever had in my lifetime. Ana looked at me and asked me what was wrong. This brisket was so good I felt like I was having an orgasm. Oh, it was so good. Damn, that brisket was so good.

No one has surpassed the taste of the brisket I had at Franklin's BBQ. At least, I haven't come across another brisket that was even close. This, again, is my opinion. Please go try Franklin's BBQ brisket and numerous other BBQ restaurants in the Austin, Texas, area. This City is BBQ Heaven.

Franklin's Meats: Brisket Slices, Pulled Pork, Pork Ribs, Sausage, Ranch Style Beans and Coleslaw.

DUKE SAYS, "THANK YOU."

CONCLUSION

I have concluded my recommendations on how to prepare and cook/smoke a Texas-style BBQ Brisket. I hope you and your family enjoyed this book as much as I enjoyed writing this book. I hope my book helps you cook your next brisket with confidence. I know your next brisket after reading this book will be awesome. Have a beer and enjoy the cooking/smoking process. If you found this book helpful, Duke, Ana, and I would be very thankful and appreciative if you left a favorable review. "Always be humble and kind to all you meet." Keep cooking.

RESOURCES

Heathcott, A. (2023, November 15). The history of Brisket. Allegro Marinade. https://allegromarinade.com/history-of-brisket/#:~:text=The%20origin%20of%20Brisket%20may%20not%20be%20what,Jewish%20holidays%20such%20as%20Hannukah%2C%20Shabbat%2C%20and%20Passover. What's your beef – prime, choice or select? (2013, January 28). USDA.

https://www.usda.gov/media/blog/2013/01/28/whats-your-beef-prime-choice-or-select Bomb Brisket: A Beginner's guide to BBQ's most legendary cut: Logan, Tibor: 9798342053815: Amazon.com: Books. (n.d.).

My Book What's your beef – prime, choice or select? (2013, January 28). USDA.

https://www.usda.gov/media/blog/2013/01/28/whats-your-beef-prime-choice-or-select The Brisket chronicles: how to barbecue, braise, smoke, and cure the world's most epic cut of meat (Steven Raichlen Barbecue Bible Cookbooks): Raichlen, Steven: 9781523505487: Amazon.com: Books. (n.d.).

My Book Franklin Barbecue: A Meat-Smoking Manifesto [A Cookbook]: Franklin, Aaron, Mackay, Jordan: 9781607747208: Amazon.com: Books. (n.d.).

My Book Barrel Smoker & Charcoal Grills | Pit Barrel® Cooker Co. (n.d.). Pit Barrel Cooker.

https://pitbarrelcooker.com/?msclkid=199760a4317b1511816307e22dd6cf73&utm_source=bing&utm_medium=cpc&utm_campaign=QT%20-%20Trademark%20-%20Exact&utm_term=pit%20barrel%20smoker&utm_content=general MSN. (n.d.).

https://www.msn.com/en-us/lifestyle/shopping/pit-boss-vs-traeger-who-makes-the-better-pellet-grill/ar-AA1qsD3m?ocid=msedgdhp&pc=U531&cvid=0b7074ac14134ded9099111e0b42d7ca&ei=13 Pit Boss Grills | Wood Pellet Grills | Flat Top Griddles | BBQ Smokers. (n.d.). Pit Boss Grills.

https://pitboss-grills.com/?irclickid=2vqWwvWcOxyKUc-zI3U-eUocUkCQcOz9pTpP1w0&irgwc=1 Oklahoma Joe's®. (n.d.). Home page. https://www.oklahomajoes.com/

Ballistic bbq website - Bing. (n.d.-b). Bing. https://www.bing.com/search?qs=MT&pq=ballistic+bbq&sk=CSYN1AS1&sc=8-13&q=ballistic+bbq+website&cvid=7d655b66a7fa43a888ae845e52db802b&gs_lcrp=EgRlZGdlKgYIARAAGEAyBggAEEUYOTIGCAEQABhAMgYIAhAAGEAyBggDEAAYQDIGCAQQABhAMgYIBRAAGEAyBggGEAAYQNIBCDY3ODhqMGo5qAIIsAIB&FORM=ANAB01&adppc=EDGEESS&

BBQ PIT BOYS VIDEOS - Bing. (n.d.). Bing. https://www.bing.com/search?q=BBQ+PIT+BOYS+VIDEOS&cvid=80566fbfdecb44d6b0c6896c287bb31d&gs_lcrp=EgRlZGdlKgYIABBFGDkyBggAEEUYOTIGCAEQRRg80gEIOTk5MWowajSoAgawAgE&FORM=ANAB01&adppc=EDGEESS&PC=U531

Smoke master d youtube - Bing. (n.d.). Bing. https://www.bing.com/search?q=smoke+

master+d+youtube&cvid=97d5203ee6854621b832c9a0686ed1ac&gs_lcrp=EgRl ZGdlKgYIABBFGDkyBggAEEUYOTIGCAEQABhAMgYIAhAAGEAyBgg DEAAYQDIGCAQQABhAMgYIBRAAGEAyBggGEAAYQDIGCAcQABhAMgYICB adppc=EDGEESS&PC=U531

Titan stainless steel grills - Bing. (n.d.). Bing. https://www.bing.com/search?q=titan+ stainless+steel+grills&cvid=4b6d5c10b38b4fa8a33cc8a1248ce755&gs_lcrp=EgRl ZGdlKgYIABBFGDkyBggAEEUYOTIGCAEQABhAMgYIAhAAGEAyBgg DEAAYQDIGCAQQABhAMgYIBRAAGEAyBggGEAAYQDIGCAcQABhAMgYICB adppc=EDGEESS&PC=U531

Mad Scientist BBQ. (n.d.). [Video]. https://www.youtube.com/c/madscientistbbq.

Arnie Tx. (n.d.). [Video]. https://www.youtube.com/channel/UCnxOJ_Un-QF_KYqbPRAfLNw.

ACKNOWLEDGMENTS

Thank you to General Manager "Taylor" and the staff at Rudy's Country Store and Bar-B-Que located at 209 W. Nolana Loop, Pharr, Texas 78577. "It was my pleasure and honor to make great Bar-B-Que for all Texans to enjoy."

ABOUT THE AUTHOR JOHN W. DAVIS

I was born and raised in Southern California in a community located in the southeastern area of San Diego, known as "Emerald Hills." I was a child who was given up for adoption and placed into foster care. I was given up for adoption by a young mother in her early twenties (20s), who had an additional four (4) children she also had to provide for. I'm thankful I was given up for adoption because it changed my life for the better.

I was premature, sickly, and was being tossed around to any foster home that would take me. My life changed when I was placed into a foster home managed by Howard and Viola Davis.

The Davis Family would later adopt me and call me their son. An honor I hold dear each day of my life. I became the man I am today due to the guidance my parents gave me growing up. I was taught at a young age to have faith in God because God was real.

I hope you enjoy this book. If you took the time out of your busy schedule to read my book, I thank you from the bottom of my heart. Be humble and kind to all you meet. Forgive those who have done you wrong (Luke 23:34).

May God bless you and yours and always keep you safe. Peace.

Duke is dog-tired.

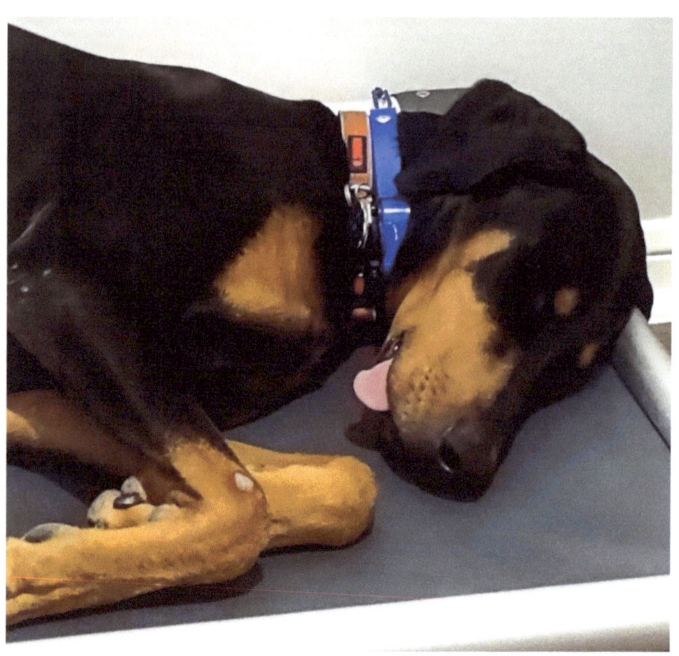